Postcards from the Past

SOMERSET PUBS

Andrew Swift & Kirsten Elliott

AKEMAN PRESS

Published by Akeman Press, 58 Minster Way, Bath BA2 6RL
www.akemanpress.com

ISBN 0 9546138 6 4
ISBN13 9780954613860

Front cover: The back of this postcard of the **Queen's Arms** at Wraxall near Ditcheat bears the date 1914 and a list of names: Will Bryant, Herb Bryant, Walt Spirrel, Queenie & Winnie Rood, Martha & Twin. Nothing more. It is an extraordinary photograph: a young man is going off to war, the driver of the cart is ready to depart, the landlord of the pub, having made his farewells, is about to go back indoors. For a moment, everything stops. Then, with the scene recorded for posterity, the driver shakes the reins, the cart trundles off and the landlord closes the door behind him. Although the world captured on this postcard was shattered forever by the Great War, the Queen's Arms, six miles south of Shepton Mallet on the A37, is still open. Although much extended, and barely recognisable as the same building, it still provides a traditional welcome and is one of the most popular dining pubs in the area.

Back cover: Drinkers enjoy a barrel of beer from Frome Breweries – much of it served in pottery mugs – at the **Selwood Inn** in Frome. John Wilcox, who can be seen holding the tray, ran the inn, at the junction of Berkley Road and Rodden Road, with his wife Fanny, from around 1890 to around 1930. After they retired to Rose Cottage in Clink, the inn was demolished and a house built on the site.

Frontispiece: The **Red Lion** in Shepton Mallet Market Place was once one of the town's top inns. On this postcard from around 1910, timetables for the Somerset & Dorset and Great Western Railways, both of which served the town, can be seen on its walls. A century on, Shepton's railways are no more than a fading memory and, although the building which once housed the Red Lion has survived, it is now home to 'a children's indoor soft play area.'

Opposite page: The **Ship Inn** at Porlock, believed to date from 1290, is one of the best-known pubs in the county. Famous visitors have included the poets Robert Southey and Samuel Taylor Coleridge. Southey penned a sonnet in the Ship and has a corner dedicated to his memory, while local legend has it that the 'person from Porlock' who disturbed Coleridge during the writing of Kubla Khan was from the Ship and wanted him to settle his tab. Just west of the inn, a 1 in 4 hill climbs to the dizzy heights of Exmoor and on into Devon. There is surely no better place than this splendid old inn to start our pub crawl round Somerset.

Printed by Short Run Press, Exeter

INTRODUCTION

This is the first in a series of books featuring English pubs as they looked a century or so ago. The earliest photographs date from the 1870s, the latest from the 1960s. The majority, however, are picture postcards published just before the First World War, the same time that Cecil Sharp was cycling round the county collecting folk songs. Most of the singers he met were elderly, the last exponents of a centuries-old tradition. If he, and others like him, had not recorded their songs when they did, they would have been lost forever. In a similar way, local postcard photographers, casting around for subjects to feature on their cards, captured and memorialised a way of life on the verge of extinction.

It was a world profoundly different from ours, yet, although we may imagine it to have been a golden age, for contemporaries it was a period of immense change. Horse power was giving way to the internal combustion engine; in the countryside it was a time of depopulation, unemployment and poverty.

Yet, while the trade that had sustained coaching inns was long gone, village pubs were still fulfilling the role they had done for centuries. Their customers almost invariably lived within walking – or riding – distance, and they relied on wet sales for the bulk, if not all, of their income.

Since then, pubs in both town and country have undergone a revolution – a revolution, which in many cases has ended either in closure or in transformation into something our ancestors would struggle to recognise. While pubs such as Eli's at Huish Episcopi or the Seymour Arms at Witham Friary have seen relatively few changes, many others – from award-winning gastropubs to family-friendly eateries – now rely on food for the bulk of their income.

This book covers the historic county of Somerset. The selection of photos has been dictated by the availability of archive images. This has ensured a representative randomness, in which humble beerhouses rub shoulders with grand coaching inns. Over 140 pubs are featured, around three-quarters of them still open. Some, from the outside at least, look much as they did a century ago; others have changed almost beyond recognition. A few have disappeared; some have been rebuilt.

If your favourite pub isn't featured, it's because we don't have an old photograph of it. We hope one day to publish a follow-up volume, with photographs that have turned up in the interim, so if you have any old pictures of pubs in Somerset – or anywhere else for that matter – please get in touch.

Thanks go to Julian Litchfield, Brenda Mahany, Eileen Pittard, Mark Steeds, Jack Sweet, Phil Whitmarsh, and everyone else who provided information.

We hope you enjoy this virtual pub crawl around Somerset as much as we enjoyed compiling it.

Andrew Swift & Kirsten Elliott

The **Queen's Head** in Minehead looked distinctly worse for wear when the postcard above was published around 1906, the year that Cecil Sharp came here to collect songs such as Spanish Ladies and Dashing Away with the Smoothing Iron from Captain Lewis, one of his most prolific contributors. Today, rebuilt and revamped, with a listing in the Good Beer Guide and regular beer festivals, the new Queen's Head, seen on the left, is a far more attractive proposition.

Despite many changes and a new name, the **Rock Inn** at Bridgetown, seen here around 1910, is still recognisable today. Built in the 1760s as a staging post on the road from Dulverton to Dunster, it has an idyllic setting in the Exe valley. With a cricket ground across the river, the Badger's Holt (as it is now called) is a favourite rendezvous for cricket teams, and a popular watering hole for residents of and visitors to this remote but beautiful corner of Somerset.

Walter Lettey was the landlord of the **Foresters' Arms** at Dunster when this postcard was published around 1909. Although believed to date from the eighteenth century, the Foresters' owes its present appearance to a nineteenth-century rebuild. By then, Dunster's illustrious history as a weaving centre was well and truly over. Years of stagnation meant that the heart of the village had hardly changed for centuries. It was this quaintness that led to Dunster's reinvention as a tourist honeypot, a role it still fulfils admirably today, with the Foresters' just one of the inns vying for visitors' trade.

By the time this postcard of the **Lion Inn** at Timberscombe was sent to Bath in August 1962, Arnold & Hancock's Brewery had been taken over by Usher's of Trowbridge and the breweries at Taunton and Wiveliscombe closed down. Although the Lion, which is believed to date from around 1600, is still going strong today, the thatched cottage behind it has disappeared.

The **Rest & Be Thankful** was an appropriate name for this early nineteenth-century coaching inn at Wheddon Cross on the road from Dulverton to Dunster. At almost a thousand feet above sea level, Wheddon Cross is the highest village on Exmoor. On the approaches to it, able-bodied coach passengers had to get out and walk, to make life easier for the horses. A pint of ale would have been very welcome – as would a roaring fire, especially in the depths of winter. Today, the inn is still a favourite stopping-off point for travellers, as well as a popular centre for walkers exploring the moor.

Dating back to the seventeenth century, the Good Pub Guide-listed **Royal Oak** at Withypool on Exmoor has seen many distinguished visitors over the years. RD Blackmore wrote part of Lorna Doone here, and in 1944, after reviewing American troops on Exmoor, General Eisenhower stopped by for a drink. More recently, in 2006, Prince William dined at the inn with friends after a hard day's hunting. When this postcard was published in the 1930s, the landlord of the Royal Oak was Maxwell Knight, the spymaster and broadcaster upon whom Ian Fleming based the character of M.

The **Royal Oak** at Winsford is seen here in the early 1920s, when horse-drawn transport was beginning to give way to the car. Its picturesque setting in the Exe valley has made the Royal Oak one of the best-known inns in Somerset. Built in the seventeenth century as a farmhouse, and extended in the nineteenth when it became an inn, the nonchalance with which this vintage car has been parked is something today's visitors may well envy as they hunt for a parking space. Changes to the inn – at least externally – have been minimal: the tall pine tree and the fence have gone, the porches and lean-to have been thatched, but that is about all.

Like the Royal Oak, the **New Inn** at Brompton Regis in the Brendon Hills was a farm before it was an inn; unlike the Royal Oak, it remained a working farm, with a room set aside for selling beer and cider. Kelly's 1902 Directory lists Fanny Kelly, whose name appears beside the door on this postcard, as a farmer and beer retailer. The inn burnt down in the 1930s, and, although the building that replaced it is still known as New Inn Farm, you now need to look elsewhere for alcoholic refreshment.

The **Egremont Hotel** in Williton is one of Somerset's most recent pub casualties. Opened as the Blue Anchor in the seventeenth century, it was renamed the Coach & Horses in 1720. In the early nineteenth century, it was rebuilt and renamed the Wyndham Arms. Finally, in 1843, it became the Egremont Hotel, after the 4th Earl of Egremont who lived at nearby Orchard Wyndham. With its cobbled courtyard, Regency ballroom and wood-panelled restaurant (not to mention a bar specialising in farmhouse cider), it was a very traditional establishment. Sadly, it has now been converted to flats.

The railway reached Washford in 1874, when the line from Taunton to Watchet was extended to Minehead. By the 1930s, with the branch at its busiest, the **Railway Inn** next to Washford station was rebuilt. In the 1960s, as the road past the hotel became busier, however, the line behind it was gradually run down. It closed in 1971, but the hotel stayed open, ready for the reopening of the line by the West Somerset Railway Association five years later. Today, the preserved line is one of the county's top visitor attractions, and the inn – now renamed the Washford Inn – is on hand to greet visitors eager for a whiff of the golden age of steam.

The **Hood Arms** at Kilve, seen here with a horse-drawn coach about to depart, was already over two centuries old when Edward Thomas stayed here in March 1913. 'Day was not dead but sleeping', he wrote later. 'Only when I lay in bed did I recognise the two sounds that made the murmurous silence of Kilve – the whisper of its brook, and the bleat of sheep very far off.' The inn has changed little, but the growth of motor transport – already evident in the 1930s photograph on the left – has put paid to that 'murmurous stillness'.

The **Limpet Shell** at Lilstock is perhaps Somerset's most profoundly lost pub. These two cards by HH Hole of Williton, postmarked 1907 and 1932 respectively, show it before and after abandonment. Sir John Acland established a harbour here around 1820 to import coal from Wales and send pit props and lime back. Around 1860, a pier was built and pleasure steamers began calling. The harbour was abandoned in the 1920s and today it is almost impossible to see where the buildings of this tiny settlement once stood.

The **Bicknoller Inn** in the western foothills of the Quantocks is still thatched and little changed since the postcard above was published in the 1920s. Its situation on a back road has also meant that its rural character has not been compromised. The postcard on the left shows the bar in the 1960s. Although a new restaurant has opened since then, it is still very much a village pub, where traditional pastimes like skittles and darts sit happily alongside untraditional ones like boules.

Built of wattle and daub, with the date of 1638 picked out in sheep-knuckle bones on the floor of its bar, the **Butcher's Arms** at Carhampton still has a cider house and orchard at the back, where a wassail, including the singing of the Carhampton Wassail Song (to keep evil spirits from the cider apples), is held every January. The postcard above dates from the 1930s, when the road past the pub was still relatively traffic free; the card on the right shows it in the 1950s.

WH Griffiths was the landlord of the **Plough Inn** at Holford when this photograph was taken around 1920. In 1912, Leonard and Virginia Woolf spent their honeymoon here, returning two years later for a holiday. Unfortunately, the charms of the Quantocks failed to work their magic on the second occasion and Leonard had to restrain his wife from jumping out of the train on the way home. Today, the trees that once surrounded the Plough have gone and traffic roars past on the A39, but, with fancy shutters and a new porch, and a growing reputation for food and real ale, the inn looks in a lot better shape than it did in the early twentieth century.

The **Castle Inn** at Huish Champflower doubled as the village post office when this card was published in the 1940s. The building has hardly changed, apart from the addition of a porch around the front door, but cider and stamps are no longer sold, as it is now a private house. A high fence and tall trees screen it from the road, and only the sign bracket on the right remains to remind passers-by there was once a pub in this tiny village hidden high in the hills north-west of Wiveliscombe.

The **Greyhound** at Stogursey bore the logo of Starkey's Brewery when this postcard was published in the 1940s. Long a familiar sight in Somerset and Devon, it started to disappear after the company, with breweries in Bridgwater and Tiverton, and around 400 pubs, was acquired by Whitbread's in 1962. Only a few examples now survive. That on the Greyhound has, like most others, been painted out. The Greyhound, however, is still very much open and now has a signboard hanging from that ornate wrought-iron bracket.

The **Carew Arms** at Crowcombe, on the south-western slopes of the Quantocks, dates back over 400 years. Originally known as the Three Lions (after the three lions on the Carew coat of arms), it acquired its present name in 1814. Despite a large extension at the back, the front is still much as it was when this postcard was published the best part of a century ago. Listed in the Good Pub Guide and the Good Beer Guide, some regulars can still remember when the local doctor held surgeries in the flagstone-floored public bar.

Wiveliscombe, eleven miles west of Taunton on the road to Barnstaple, was an important coaching town; in 1813, it had twelve large inns. The **White Hart**, first recorded in 1807, looked decidedly down at heel when this postcard was published in the early twentieth century. The coaching trade had long since disappeared and once prosperous inns like the White Hart relied almost exclusively on local trade. Today, after a sympathetic makeover, the inn, with a popular restaurant and 16 bedrooms, has bounced back with a vengeance.

One inn that didn't bounce back was the **Lion**. All that remains to indicate it was once one of Wiveliscombe's top coaching inns is the figure of a lion over the archway leading to the coachyard. The narrow streets of this historic town, once on the main road from Taunton to North Devon, have, since the opening of a bypass, returned to something approaching the calm apparent in the 1930s postcard view above.

In the early 1900s, the **Three Horseshoes** at Langley Marsh near Wiveliscombe was reroofed, extended and hung with two types of tiles, giving it a vaguely Home Counties look. Today, as the photograph on the left shows, the tiles have gone, revealing the red sandstone underneath. Despite the changes – and listings in the Good Beer and Good Pub Guides – it is a resolutely traditional pub, with shove ha'penny and a skittle alley, and a meeting place for the local cricket team and vintage car enthusiasts.

Almost a thousand feet above sea level, on the southern flank of the Brendon Hills, the **Lowtrow Cross Inn** is believed to date from the sixteenth century. On the turnpike road from Watchet to Bampton, opened in 1765, the inn has long been a welcoming sight for travellers. Although it has been extended, lost its garden wall, and has a large campsite in an adjoining field, the Lowtrow Cross Inn would still be recognisable to regulars who knew it when William Sloley was the landlord a century or so ago.

Nestling in the hidden countryside between the Quantocks and Exmoor, the **New Inn** at Halse, an eighteenth-century coaching inn, not only provides food and accommodation, but also brews its own beer. The curiously-named Somerset (Electric) Brewery, founded in 2003, has been succeeded by the Taunton Vale Brewery, which opened in late 2006. Despite frenetic activity on the brewing front, the scene has hardly changed in the 70 years or so since this postcard was published. The inn may have a new sign, but the lanes are still as narrow, the vegetation still as verdant and the pub every bit as popular.

The **Tynte Arms** at Enmore, west of Bridgwater in the foothills of the Quantocks, opened as a beerhouse, probably in the old Pound Cottage, in the 1840s. By the time this postcard was published in the 1920s, there was a post office and general store at the back of the pub. Today, much extended, the Tynte Arms has decorative shutters and the shop has been converted to accommodation. Rogers' Ales & Stout, advertised in enamel lettering on the window on the left, came from a brewery on Jacob Street in Bristol, which closed in 1935 after acquisition by H&G Simonds of Reading.

The **Rock Inn** at Waterrow in the Brendon Hills has changed very little since this postcard was published early last century. On the coach road from Taunton to Barnstaple, a few miles west of Wiveliscombe, it has an idyllic location in the steep-sided valley of the River Tone. Stagecoaches had been supplanted by cars by the time this photograph was taken, but there is little indication in this bucolic scene of how heavy traffic through Waterrow would one day become. The opening of the North Devon Link Road in 1989 has, however, restored something of the tranquillity captured in this photograph.

This postcard from around 1907 shows the annual procession of the Nether Stowey Ladies' Friendly Society. After a church service, the women headed for the **Rose & Crown** – on the right – for tea. The procession still takes place, although tea is now taken at the village hall. The Good Beer Guide-listed Rose & Crown looks much the same today, although the George Inn next door looks very different, having had tiles applied to its front wall.

Samuel Taylor Coleridge wrote The Rime of the Ancient Mariner and Kubla Khan while staying in the cottage opposite Nether Stowey's **First & Last Inn** in 1797-98. Later, the cottage became Moore's Coleridge Cottage Inn, with a reputation as 'the worst conducted public house in Stowey.' By the time this postcard was published in the early 1900s, Coleridge's Cottage had become a museum. The First & Last, renamed the Ancient Mariner in 1982, is still open, but, as the picture on the left shows, now sports a half-timbered look.

As the photograph on the right shows, half-timbering is also in evidence at North Petherton's **Compass Inn**. The original building, seen above around 1905, has had a major extension, incorporating the old lean-to, built at the front. The massive buttress beside the chimney, however, remains. The pub was owned by Starkey, Knight & Ford's (later shortened to Starkey's) of Bridgwater and Tiverton. Before teaming up with Knight and Ford, Thomas Starkey owned a brewery and malthouse on Fore Street in North Petherton.

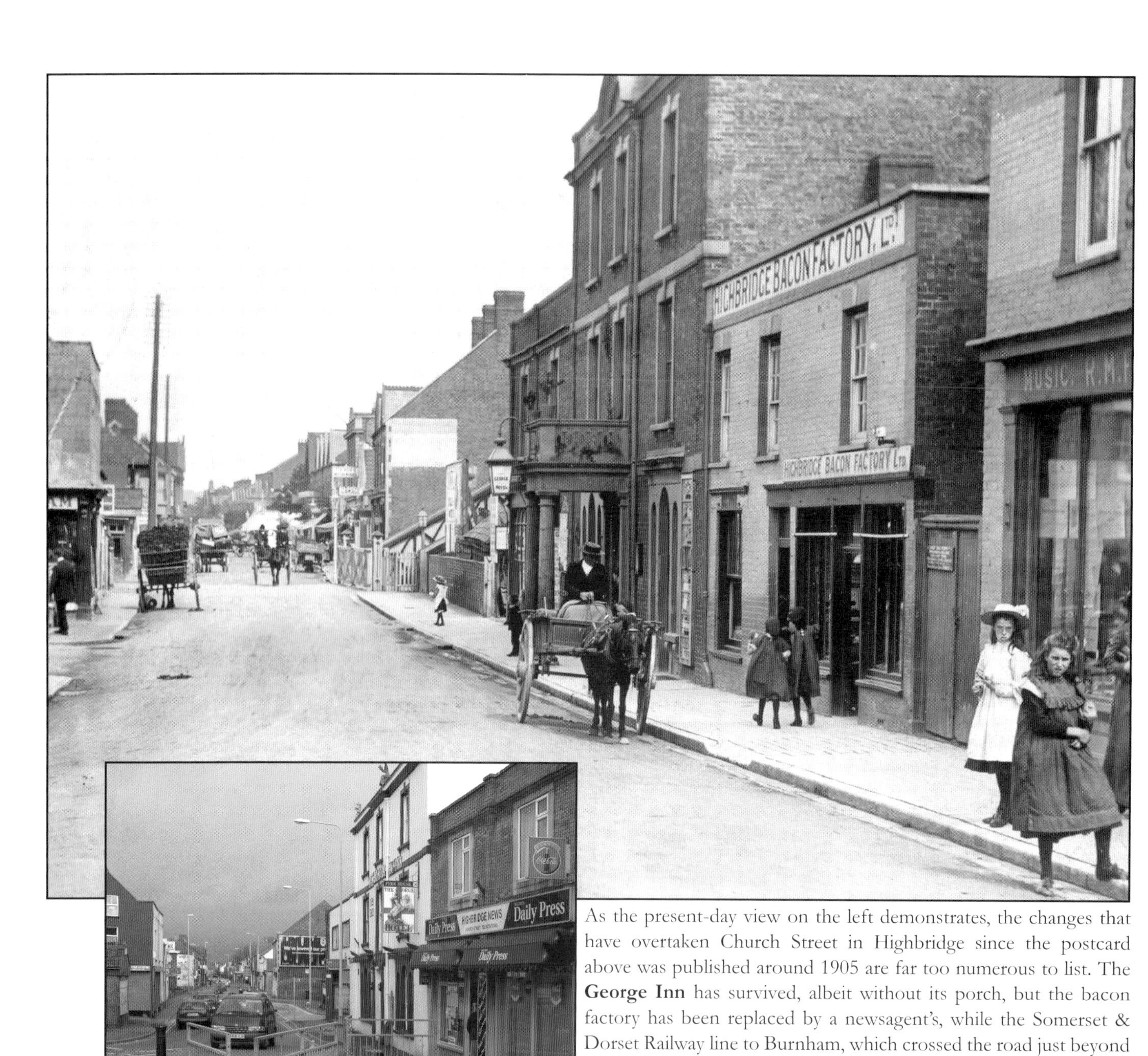

As the present-day view on the left demonstrates, the changes that have overtaken Church Street in Highbridge since the postcard above was published around 1905 are far too numerous to list. The **George Inn** has survived, albeit without its porch, but the bacon factory has been replaced by a newsagent's, while the Somerset & Dorset Railway line to Burnham, which crossed the road just beyond the inn, closed as long ago as 1962.

Despite changes to its doors and windows, the **Cross Rifles** in Bridgwater today is clearly the same pub that appeared on the postcard above almost a century ago. Located to the north of the town, where the roads to Bath and Bristol diverged, it was not only a busy coaching inn, but also attracted local trade as the town expanded in the nineteenth century. Today, with the flag of St George flying proudly from its roof, it is one of the town's top music venues.

Facing south down the A38 as the road curves into town, the **Highbridge Hotel**, now known as the Highbridge Inn, with its elegant doric portico, has been a familiar sight to travellers for over 200 years. Dating from the eighteenth century but remodelled in the nineteenth, the semi-circular-headed stairlight above the porch is its most striking feature, transforming what would otherwise be a run-of-the-mill building into something memorable. George's Bristol Brewery, which owned the hotel when this postcard was published in the 1950s, was founded in the early eighteenth century. By 1961, when Courage's took it over, it owned 1,459 pubs.

'Dear Ike, Do you remember this place? Known to me as "Woolley's retreat"! Beer and skittles, what ho! Am quite an expert at both, thanks to your early training. That's old Tommy standing in the doorway. He wishes to be remembered to you.' So runs the message on this card of the **Fox & Goose** at Brent Knoll, sent to Isaac Wheal in Hong Kong in July 1906. Tommy was Tom Bowgin, the landlord. Today, traffic roars past on the A38 yards away from the front door, the doric portico has disappeared under a single-storey extension stretching the length of the building, pebble-dash covers the brickwork, and a new hotel and conference centre has been built on the left.

The **White Lion** at Woolavington is seen here on a postcard published in the early 1900s. Open by 1679, when it was known as the Phoenix, it was renamed the White Lion in 1788 and closed in 1913. The building is still there, half hidden by the trees that have sprung up in its front garden, but, unless you knew, you'd never guess it was once the village inn. Old postcards often raise tantalising questions. There's no problem with the group of children on the right; such groups were an occupational hazard for local photographers. But why is that boy sitting by himself in the gutter on the other side of the road?

Whitby, Light & Lane of Bridgwater published this postcard of the **Rose & Crown** at East Lyng in the 1920s. Open by 1709, and originally known as the Lyng Inn, it was renamed the Rose & Crown around 1786. The trellis has gone from the front wall, the windows have been painted black, the outhouse on the right has made way for a car park and the steps have been skewed so that patrons aren't disgorged onto a busy road, but otherwise the Rose & Crown, now listed in the Good Pub Guide, has changed very little.

JA Willing was the landlord of the **Brent Knoll Inn** at East Brent when this postcard was sent to South Wales in 1931. Although the pub is still open and its basic structure has survived intact, so many changes have been wrought since then that the pub and its surroundings are virtually unrecognisable. But, as the number of cars in the present-day picture indicates, it is even more popular now than it was then.

In AD878, King Alfred withdrew to Athelney to rally his forces after losing a battle with Danish forces. The successful counter-attack he subsequently launched was one of the most decisive events in England's struggle towards nationhood. Despite its illustrious past, Athelney today seems a place that history has passed by. The **Athelney Inn**, seen above around 1880 during one of the village's frequent inundations, has long closed and, as the present-day view shows, is now a private house.

The local militia fire off a volley, accompanied by the regimental band, outside the Market House in Castle Cary early last century. Doubtless some of the crowd who gathered to witness this stirring spectacle nipped into the **Angel Inn**, on the far side of the square, for a quick drink once it was all over. The Angel, one of several coaching inns in the town, closed in the 1960s and is now Chinn's Antiques. A beer engine used in the Angel has survived, however, and can be seen in the museum on the first floor of the Market House.

Somerton is one of the oldest towns in the county. Originally known as Sea-Mere Town because it was built on an island surrounded by water, it is believed to have given its name to the county of Somerset. In the eighteenth century it was an important coaching town, and the **Red Lion**, built of blue lias stone with Ham stone dressings in the 1770s, was one of its top inns. Today, not only have the coaches gone; the trains no longer stop at Somerton either, and the Red Lion has been converted to flats.

Two more of Somerton's coaching inns – the **White Hart** (originally the Bear) and the **Globe** – can be seen on this postcard from the 1920s. Both are still open and, superficially at least, appear much the same today, although the splendid carving of the white hart has sadly gone. Although the White Hart looks eighteenth century, behind that façade lurk traces of a medieval building.

Our final view of Somerton is an evocative shot of the **New Commercial Hotel** in New Street from around 1910. Now renamed the Somerton Hotel, it retains its old porch, and, apart from a creeper covering the lias stone wall, looks much as it did a century ago. The most significant change has been the conversion of Tarrant's Grocer's into a private house.

The **Black Swan** in North Street, Langport is seen here on a postcard from 1905. The name of this historic town on the River Parrett recalls the days when it was an inland port. As late as the mid-nineteenth century, it handled 40,000 tons of goods a year. The Black Swan, an eighteenth-century rebuild of an earlier building, is still open, but looks very different. The roof has been repitched, a straight lintel inserted into the semi-circular-headed archway, the building beyond the pub demolished to make way for a car park and the building beyond that replaced by a modern building.

A lady in a carriage passes the **Newtown Inn**, on the northern edge of Langport, around 1910. Situated on a ridge looking westward across the Somerset Levels, the inn had one of the finest views in the county. Built, unlike most of the houses around it, of red brick, it has long been a private house. Mitchell & Toms' Brewery, which owned the Newtown Inn, closed in 1937 following takeover by Brutton's of Yeovil.

The **Rose & Crown** at Huish Episcopi near Langport is one of Somerset's best-known and best-loved pubs. The boy on this postcard from around 1907 is probably one of William Slade's sons, both of whom were killed in the First World War. The pub eventually passed to William's daughter and son-in-law, Eli Scott. Today, Eli's daughter, Eileen is the landlady, and the pub – still known as Eli's – looks much the same as it did a century ago. There is no bar counter: you walk straight into a tap room, with beer and cider served from the barrel, and a warren of tiny rooms leading off. It was almost certainly at Eli's that Cecil Sharp met the 66-year-old Emma Overd one evening in 1904. She lived across the road on Knapp's Lane and was, he records, sitting outside a pub when he pulled up on his bike and told her he was collecting traditional songs. At this, she jumped to her feet and danced round him 'with the utmost vigour', shouting that her beau had come. Among the songs she sang that evening were The Wraggle Taggle Gipsies and Bruton Town, which have become two of the best-loved folk songs of all time. A monthly singers' night at Eli's still keeps up the tradition so energetically embodied by Mrs Overd.

For a pub so close to the magnificent tower of Taunton's St James's Church to be called anything other than the **Ring of Bells** could never seriously have been on the cards. This traditional local has hardly changed since this postcard was published in the 1950s, although you'd be unlikely to find these sort of vehicles parked outside today. A couple of minutes walk from the county cricket ground, and open all day during home matches, the tranquillity of its beer garden is rarely disturbed by anything more dramatic than a distant 'howzat'. Evenings, however, are somewhat livelier, with karaoke sessions and regular skittle matches.

Books have taken over from beer with a vengeance in Taunton. Not only does Waterstone's occupy the old County Hotel; the site of **Bryant's Wine and Spirit Vaults** in Fore Street is now occupied by WH Smith's. This splendid postcard, dating from the 1920s, is a reminder of the days when off licences delivered by bike. Until comparatively recently, the distinction between off licences and pubs was often blurred. Many pubs had a thriving takeaway trade, while wine & spirit vaults often allowed customers to drink on the premises. There are still pubs called the Wine Vaults in Shepton Mallet, Yeovil and Bath, but Bryant's of Taunton is now but a fond memory.

The whitewashed **White Hart** at Corfe, in the lee of the Blackdown Hills, still looks much as it did when this postcard was published in the early 1900s. The loss of render on the side wall and the blocking up of the gateway at the front are just about all there is to show for a century of change. Popular for food, the White Hart is still very much a village pub, with real fires and – not surprisingly given its proximity to Taunton Racecourse – much talk of horses.

The garden wall may have been sacrificed to make way for car parking, but otherwise the **White Horse** at Bradford on Tone looks much as it did when this postcard was published a century ago. Listed in the Good Beer Guide and famous for food, with its garden boasting a petanque court and its forecourt hosting Morris Dancing on New Year's Day, the White Horse is, despite many changes, a traditional village inn – although what the characters on this card would make of the Fawlty Towers theme nights is anybody's guess.

The eighteenth-century **Hatch Inn** at Hatch Beauchamp, east of the Blackdown Hills, is still open, with accommodation, roaring log fires and a listing in the Good Beer Guide. The distinctive full-height canted bays were added in the nineteenth century. It still looks much as it did in this view from the late 1920s, when the proud owner of a new Flatnose Morris parked outside the front door. The replacement of the window on the far left by a door is the only major change in the last 80 years.

On 1 May 1843, the **Beam Bridge Inn** near Wellington suddenly found itself one of the busiest places in the county when Brunel established the western terminus of the Bristol & Exeter Railway a few yards from its front door. As the only building of consequence in the area, it effectively became the railhead for all points west, and extra stables were built to cope with demand as trainloads of passengers fought for carriages to carry them onward. Twelve months later, a 1092-yard-long tunnel opened under Whiteball Hill and the line was extended to Exeter. Beam Bridge station closed and the inn slipped back into obscurity, its tranquillity broken only by trains rushing past on their way west. Today, much extended, the inn has found a new role as a conference centre and hotel.

The **Bishopswood Inn** – now the Candlelight Inn – lies a few hundred yards from the Devon border high in the Blackdown Hills. With the River Yarry flowing through its garden, it has one of the most enviable locations in the county. The render on its walls has gone, porches have been added, the grass has been cut back to make way for a car park, and the tree is 80 years older than when this photograph was taken, but the Candelight, with its low-beams and Good Beer Guide listing, is still a characterful and popular village inn.

The old part of the **York Inn** at Churchinford dates from the late sixteenth or early seventeenth century. The inn, which was extended in the nineteenth century, is still open, but since this photograph was taken in the early 1950s its thatch has been replaced by tiles, the Starkey's sign has been replaced by a splendid painting of vegetables, and wisteria has covered much of the once-whitewashed wall. Although still very much a village local, its reputation for food and hospitality have earned it a place in several pub guides.

Wellington, in the far south-west of the county, was once an important coaching centre. Fore Street, on the main route into the town from the south, has changed little since this postcard was published a century ago, although the **Squirrel Inn**, dating from around 1672, closed in 1972. Today, its brick façade covered with pebbledash, it is the town's museum, although, with its signboard still bearing the image of a squirrel, it is still recognisable as a former inn.

James Tristram was landlord of the **King's Arms** in Wellington High Street when this postcard was published around 1910. Although still open, this pub has changed so much that it is virtually unrecognisable. The archway into the courtyard has been filled in, the brickwork covered with stucco and elaborate mouldings inserted between the windows. Now resplendent in red and cream, and with more than a hint of art-deco cinema design, the King's Arms has come a long way since Mr Tristram stood proudly outside his inn.

When the postcard above was published around 1910, a lady cyclist had the road past the **White Horse** in South Cheriton to herself. William Hannam, seen on the left, was the landlord of this eighteenth-century inn near Wincanton for over 30 years, from around 1905 to around 1936. Although its walls have been whitewashed and the number of entrances reduced from three to two, the White Horse, with its beamed ceilings and open fireplaces, is still a traditional village pub. The road, however, is considerably busier.

The **George Inn** at Combe St Nicholas near Chard opened in 1813. The view above dates from around 1920 when Charles Venn was the landlord. After the Second World War, the pub was taken over by his son, Jack, seen in the photograph on the right. Today, not only is the road through Combe a good deal less muddy than it was in the 1920s, the Jubilee Lamp has been moved, the outhouse beyond the inn replaced by a modern building, and the George converted to a private house.

Chard, the most southerly as well as the highest town in Somerset, is some 500 feet above sea level and only a mile from the Devonshire border. Packed with historic buildings, and with a stream running down its main street, Chard has an atmosphere like no other town in the county. The **George**, dating from the late eighteenth century, is seen here around 1920. Today it is known as the Phoenix, and, although a travel agent's occupies part of the ground floor, and the first-floor windows have been remodelled, the splendid Doric porch, adorned with elaborate ironwork, has survived.

The **Choughs**, a little further up Chard's main street, is seen here on another postcard from around 1920. An inn since at least 1644, its squared flint walls, limestone quoins and Ham stone dressings exhibit a long-gone craftsmanship. Judge Jeffreys reputedly stayed here during the Bloody Assizes after the Monmouth Rebellion. Given its history, it has more than its fair share of ghostly associations, no doubt helped by the unexplained presence of a weathered tombstone, with the name Winifred carved on it, embedded in one of the fireplaces.

When a station opened at Chard Road, on the Salisbury-Exeter line, in 1863, this pub, the **Chard Road Inn**, was built next to it. Three years later, a branch opened to Chard and the station was renamed Chard Junction. The inn, however, seen here around 1907, kept its old name. The branch closed in 1962, the junction station four years later, and now the trains pass through without stopping. Renamed the Three Counties Inn, and without its ornate porch and rooftop lettering, the inn, which suffered extensive flood damage in 2000, is now a guest house.

The **Red Lion** at Crewkerne has also seen a subtle change of use since this postcard was published around 1905. Its bars are still open to the public, but today it is a Bilby's Coffee Shop. Open by 1751, and once one of the town's top coaching inns, the days when billiards could be played and a glass hearse with rubber tyres was kept out the back are long gone. Although coffee and cakes are now the order of the day, and that elaborate porch has disappeared, the building looks much the same from the outside, while inside some old stained glass windows recall more expansive times.

The Seavington Hunt meet outside the **Poulett Arms** at Lopen Head on a postcard from 1907. This pub, on a busy roundabout near South Petherton, was destroyed by fire in the mid-twentieth century and replaced by a new building, still trading as the Poulett Arms today. Nobody knows how long an inn has stood on this site. The Roman Fosse Way passed nearby and in 2001 the village of Lopen, a few hundred yards away, made national headlines when a large Roman mosaic was discovered. Earl Poulett, after whom the inn was named, lived at Hinton St George, where another pub – the Lord Poulett Arms – also bears his name.

People had started to turn up to meets in their cars by the time this postcard of the **Sparkford Inn** was published in the 1920s. Open by 1605, and known as the Punch Bowl for much of the nineteenth century, the Sparkford Inn not only doubled as a working farm, but hosted a fortnightly livestock market until the 1930s. The Sparkford Inn was also the first property acquired by the People's Refreshment Houses Association, set up in 1896 to create a network of model public houses throughout the country. The Sparkford Vale Harriers, seen on this card, were established in 1888 and amalgamated with the Blackmoor Vale Hunt in 1971.

The **Wyndham Arms** at Kingsbury Episcopi was already centuries old when this postcard was published in the early 1900s, its mullion windows and Ham stone walls testifying to a prosperity that had all but vanished. Although scenes like this seem the embodiment of lost innocence, poverty and unemployment were endemic in rural communities before the First World War, and the overwhelming impression was often one of decay. Today, Kingsbury is once again a thriving, prosperous community, and the Wyndham Arms, with its blues club and cider from nearby Burrow Hill Farm, is more popular than ever.

The **Odcombe Inn**, on the left of this 1920s postcard, may be no more than a distant memory, but the Mason's Arms in the distance – then just a humble beerhouse – has not only survived; it now has its own brewery. Listed in the Good Beer Guide, the Mason's Arms has also won accolades for its food. Odcombe, just north-west of Yeovil, may not be one of Somerset's best-known villages, but it has at least one other claim to fame: Thomas Coryate, a famous traveller who was born here in 1579, introduced the custom of eating with a fork to England.

The future Queen Victoria - then only seven months old - stayed at the **George** in Ilminster with her parents, the Duke and Duchess of Kent, en route to Sidmouth on 23 December 1819. Most of this grand eighteenth-century coaching inn, seen here in the mid-twentieth century, has now been converted into flats, called, appropriately, Victoria Court. A small pub called the George, listed in the Good Pub Guide, can still be found, however, to the left of the archway that once led to the inn yard. The building itself has changed remarkably little, the major difference being the cross braces added to stabilise the building.

Apart from an increase in traffic, Ilminster's High Street has also changed remarkably little. Ilminster is still a bustling market town, although the International Stores is now a Smile store and **Ye Olde Vine**, a Mitchell Toms house when this postcard was published in the 1930s, now forms part of Boots the Chemist.

Haselbury Plucknett, just east of Crewkerne, was once an important pilgrimage centre because of St Wulfric, an anchorite who lived here in the twelfth century. It was also to Haselbury that Cecil Sharp came in 1906 to meet Susan Williams, a 76-year-old widow who sang him songs such as The Keys of Heaven and Farewell Nancy. Mrs Williams doubtless knew the **White Horse**, seen here on a postcard from around 1930. Its brick facade may have been whitewashed, and the thatched building on the left demolished for road sidening, but the White Horse is still a vital part of the community today.

Herbert Saunders was the landlord of the **Bell** in South Petherton when this card was posted from the town in 1919. Now renamed the Brewer's Arms, it hosts two beer festivals a year, in May and August, and was runner-up in the 2007 Somerset CAMRA Pub of the Year awards. The Ham stone inn, which dates from 1622, was largely rebuilt in 1925, and the thatch replaced by asbestos cement slates, but it still looks much the same as it did 90 years ago.

John Reyland was a particularly peripatetic publican. In 1902 he was running a beerhouse in Thorney, by 1914 he had taken over one at Long Load, but in 1897 he was running the **Royal Marine** at Coat, west of Martock. Nothing underlines the decline in the rural economy in the late 1800s more graphically than this view of a once grand building being used as a beerhouse. This evocative photograph, with the Merriott carrier pausing on his rounds and the staff of the Royal Marine standing in line, gives us a glimpse of a world lost beyond recall. The building survives as a private house (with a Doric portico for added gravitas) but the way of life captured here has gone forever.

Another glimpse into a forgotten world, on a postcard from around 1905. The **New Inn** at Chiselborough, which George Hunt opened as a beerhouse in 1896, occupied a seventeenth-century Ham stone farmhouse. In a secluded valley, surrounded by five hills, Chiselborough was – and still is – a delightful spot, although its annual horse and cattle fair, established in 1257 and held on the last Thursday in October, is no more than a distant memory . The New Inn – now renamed the Cat Head Inn – looks much the same as it did a century ago, and, with a listing in the Good Pub Guide and an award-winning menu, is more popular than ever.

With its signboard jutting at a jaunty angle, the **Cow Inn** stood in the lee of Ilchester's octagonal tower. Situated at the junction of five Roman roads, Ilchester was once the second largest town in Somerset after Bath. A royal borough, it had a mint, a courthouse, a gaol, six churches, a friary, a nunnery and a leper hospital. Despite centuries of gradual decline, it was the county town until 1832, when Taunton took over. Few towns in Somerset fell so far, and so fast, as Ilchester, but few towns had so far to fall. Today, the presence of nearby RNAS Yeovilton has seen a reversal in its fortunes, while the old Cow Inn has found a new role as a private house.

The **Dolphin Inn**, resplendent in two-tone lias and Ham stone, can be seen on the left in this early twentieth-century view of Ilchester High Street. In the eighteenth and early nineteenth centuries, Ilchester's economy was kept afloat by the coaching trade. The loss of this trade in the 1840s was compounded by the avoidance of the town by the railway companies. The population slumped from 975 in 1831 to 564 in 1901. However, this decline meant that there was little development to mar one of the most interesting historic towns in Somerset. This view, for example, has hardly changed in the last century. Even better, the Dolphin is still in business.

The **Red Lion** at Bower Hinton near Martock occupied a building dating back to the seventeenth century, although records of it being licensed as an inn only go back to 1795. It closed around 1970 and, although now a private house, is in as good shape as it was when this postcard was published in the 1930s. Sadly, the building on the left – less distinguished to be sure, but almost certainly of a similar vintage – has been replaced by a modern house.

Herbert Chinnock was the landlord of the **Catash Inn** at North Cadbury when this postcard was published in the early twentieth century. The inn got its name because it is in the Hundred of Cat Ash. Hundreds were old territorial divisions, so called because they contained a hundred landowning families. Although the inn has survived virtually intact, even down to its distinctive porch, it has been extended, and now offers accommodation, along with beer, wine, cider and a popular Sunday carvery. The cottage across the road, however, has been replaced by a modern building.

This postcard view of the **Elephant & Castle** in Middle Street, Yeovil dates from the early twentieth century, when William Garlick was the landlord. After standing empty for several years, in 2003 the former inn was identified as a key site in the Yeovil Vision Town Centre Regeneration Strategy. Sold to a local businessman in 2005 and restored with the aid of a grant, work was completed in May 2006.

Probably built in the early nineteenth century, the Elephant & Castle made the transition from coaching inn to commercial hotel that so many inns failed to do. Unlike many Somerset towns, Yeovil's population grew, rather than declined, in the nineteenth century, helped by the Great Western and London & South Western Railways, which both built main lines through – or at any rate near – the town.

The **George** in Middle Street, Yeovil, a Wealden-style merchant's house with a central open hall between jettied end bays under a single roof, dated from the fifteenth century and was converted to an inn in the seventeenth century, when a floor was inserted in the central hall to make an upper room. Originally the Three Cups, it became the George in the eighteenth century. One of the oldest and most interesting inns in Somerset, it is hardly surprising that it featured on a number of picture postcards. What is surprising – to put it mildly – is that it was demolished in 1962.

Two young men stand smoking outside the **King's Arms** in Winsham around 1905. Now a familiar sight due to the smoking ban, a century ago tobacco was the almost inevitable accompaniment to ale. The idea that people would one day have to stand outside to smoke would have seemed inconceivable – as inconceivable, perhaps, as the closure not only of the King's Arms but also of the George at the top of the street. But, although both pubs are now private houses, the scene has hardly changed in a century.

The **Piper's Inn** at Ashcott is seen here around 1905, with a modern view on the left. The reason for its extraordinary appearance is unknown, but it seems likely that, in the early 1800s, the landlord decided to rebuild the seventeenth-century inn, but, not wanting to disrupt trade, tacked half of his intended building onto the side of the old inn, planning to demolish the old inn and build the other half later. Then the money ran out – or, more likely, the coaching trade collapsed – leaving the Piper's a half-rebuilt essay in building styles.

William Bull was the landlord of the **Half Moon** at Mudford, two miles outside Yeovil, when the postcard above was published around 1920. Believed to date from the seventeenth century, but drastically rebuilt in the nineteenth, the Half Moon has not only survived, but expanded. Listed in the Good Beer Guide, and with 13 en-suite bedrooms, its brick and stone have disappeared under gleaming render, while a raft of other improvements have transformed the old inn almost beyond recognition.

Any problems matching up the past and present views of the **Lamb Inn** at Lower Weare, on the A38 between Brent Knoll and Axbridge, are due to its having been demolished and replaced by a large modern pub, also called the Lamb, just out of shot to the right of the present-day picture. The site of the old inn is now covered by the new inn's car park. And whatever else may have changed since the postcard above was published in 1906, anyone standing where the gent in the flat cap was standing almost certainly wouldn't be there long.

This was Glastonbury a century ago, with the eighteenth-century **Crown** (now the Backpackers' Hostel) on the left and the **George & Pilgrims Inn** (originally a hostel for fifteenth-century pilgrims) further up the street. The postcard on the right shows Abbot Whiting's room in the George & Pilgrims around 1910. Whether a premium was payable for the room is unknown, but it is likely that modern guests would post a strongly-worded comment on Trip Advisor if they found themselves confronted by something like this.

In parts of Somerset, the Abbot of Glastonbury was once more powerful than the king (which helps to explain why the king eventually got rid of him). At Meare, a few miles west of Glastonbury, not only did he have a summer palace; this building was a monastic residence as well. After the dissolution of the monasteries, the local rector lived in it for a while before it became the Grapevine Inn. By the early twentieth century it had been renamed the **Ring O'Bells**, but today it is a further education college – just the latest chapter in the story of an ancient building in one of the most palpably medieval villages in Somerset.

Perched on a ridge above the Somerset Levels, North Curry has long been a centre of the willow industry. The village takes its name from the Celtic word 'crwy', meaning border, indicating that it once marked the frontier between Celts and Saxons. Hard to imagine that this tranquil place was once the equivalent of a demilitarised zone. This evocative postcard of the **Angel Inn** from around 1906 is, once again, a glimpse of a world we have lost, when people had time to stand and stare. The row of houses survives, but the inn is now a private house with a fancy front door. The shop has gone too, although its frontage has been preserved.

The **Waldegrave Arms** at Chewton Mendip, seen here on a postcard from the 1920s, was a large coaching inn on the road from Bath to Wells. The elaborate hood over its front door and the moulded keystones over its windows indicate that it was one of the more substantial buildings in the village. It was demolished in 1935 for road widening, but its name was transferred to a beerhouse called the Rising Sun which can be glimpsed behind the blind of the shop on the right. Now much extended, the new Waldegrave Arms is one of the best-known and most popular pubs on Mendip.

The old inn at **Rodney Stoke** burnt down in 1911 and was replaced by this superb arts-and-craft style reworking of a traditional vernacular building style. Its distinctive purple-hued sandstone came from quarries at nearby Draycott (which also supplied the stone for Temple Meads station in Bristol). Now much extended at the back, but with little change to the original building, the Rodney Stoke still has, in the words of this 1920s postcard, 'good accommodation for motorists'.

In AD878, Guthrum, King of the Danes, after being roundly defeated by King Alfred's forces, signed a treaty at Wedmore agreeing to make no further incursions into Wessex. Today, this thriving village in the Cheddar Valley is better known for an annual beer festival, a rousing harvest home and Smoked Wedmore cheese. A century ago, it was the Wedmore Band, established in 1819, that was the main attraction in the village. They played in the open at least once a week, as well as at dances, where they swapped their brass instruments for clarinets, flutes and piccolos. Here they are seen playing outside the **George Inn** around 1906.

The cellar bar of the **George** was at the cutting edge of pub design when this postcard appeared in the 1950s. This old coaching inn was propelled to fame in 1999 when, inspired by Tracey Emin's My Bed, shortlisted for that year's Turner Prize, the idea of a alternative award – the Turnip Prize – was dreamt up here one evening. Under the slogan, 'we know it's rubbish, but is it art?', locals were invited to submit entries. Since then, media coverage has led to the award becoming a standard bearer for critics of the Turner Prize. It just goes to show what can happen when you have what seems like a good idea after a night in the pub.

John Wheeler was the landlord of the **Lamb** at Worle when it appeared on the postcard above, published by Etches & Co of Bristol, in 1905. The Lamb is still open and, though recognisable, has seen many changes. A porch has been added to the central door, the two doors on either side of it have been blocked up, a row of bollards has appeared at the front, and generally it looks in much better shape. The Banwell Brewery, which owned the pub in 1905, closed four years later after being acquired by George's. The **Brewer's Arms** at Banwell, however, which stood alongside the brewery, is still open. The postcard on the right shows the Brewer's shortly before the First World War when Arthur Cock was the landlord. In an idylllic situation alongside a fast-flowing stream, it is still very much part of the local community, with charity treasure hunts and live music nights, while the stream once used for brewing beer is now the venue for an annual duck race.

Licensed as long ago as 1758, the **Old Inn** at Clevedon, on the road from Portishead to Weston, is the oldest inn in town. Once used for rent-day feasts by the Clevedon Court Estate, it looks – apart from the loss of the canted bay and the replacement of the dormer window by a chimney stack – much the same as it did when this postcard was published a century ago, although the road is a good deal busier today. Listed in the Good Beer Guide, the Old Inn has a large beer garden and also offers accommodation.

In 1895, when the lease of the **Golden Lion** at Wrington was put up for sale – for £28 a year – it had a bar, bar parlour, smoking room and commercial room. Today, the inside of the Golden Lion, like that of the Old Inn at Clevedon, has been knocked through into one large room. Like the Old Inn, however, it is still a community pub, with an annual beer festival and summer pig roast. The stonework at the far end of the pub has been covered in render, but, apart from that (and the disappearance of the sign advertising Oakhill Stout), this view has changed little since this postcard was published in the 1950s.

In this superbly mud-spattered view of the **Druids' Arms** at Stanton Drew from 1905, the landlady, Mary Johnson, stares impassively ahead, ignoring the photographer. The beerhouse only opened in the mid-1800s, but within its curtilage lies something that predates – by several millennia – everything else in this book. The two standing stones in the pub's garden form part of the second largest megalithic circle in England. Today, a ground-floor bay has been added to the building and the first-floor windows pushed up into the roof, but, despite its unique garden ornaments, the Druids' is still an unspoilt and very popular village pub.

The **Dundry Inn**, on the other hand, has seen considerable changes since this postcard was published some 60 years ago. A far bigger change had already taken place, however – the imposition of a large extension onto the original three-bay Georgian building, part of which can be seen on the right. Since then, a further extension has all but hidden the old building. One thing that hasn't changed is the pub's superb location next to St Michael's Church, with spectacular views over Bristol. The block of Dundry Stone in the foreground is the dole stone, where alms were once given to the poor of the parish.

The open road at Nailsea a century ago, with the **Queen's Head** on the right. The pub, recently renamed Bragg's Wine Bar, has changed remarkably little, but its surroundings have been transformed beyond recognition. A large brick building now stands on the other side of it; opposite, the Crown Glass Shopping Centre dominates the scene. In the foreground grass, shrubs and trees mark the point where the road has been diverted to make way for another part of the shopping centre. Nailsea's population, around 1700 when this photograph was taken, has risen to around 18,000 today. Believed to date from the sixteenth century, but rebuilt in the nineteenth, the Queen's Head must have seen many changes over the past 400 years, but few as dramatic as those of the last 50.

Parking was a lot easier in Chew Magna when this postcard was published early last century than it is today. The elegance of the golden age of motoring is epitomised by this chauffeur standing proudly by his vehicle while his employer samples the delights of the **Bear & Swan**. Externally, this Victorian inn has hardly changed in the intervening century. Inside, it has been transformed into a popular gastropub, with stripped pine and a listing in the Good Pub Guide. The Ashton Gate Brewery, which owned the pub when this photograph was taken, closed after being acquired by George's in 1931. Since 2004, however, the building once occupied by the brewery has been home to the Bristol Beer Factory.

The **Pelican**, next door to the Bear & Swan, is several centuries older. Open by 1615, it has clearly been substantially rebuilt since, and is a popular, friendly two-bar village local. Apart from the loss of the George's Brewery sign and the painting of the windows white, it has hardly changed since this postcard was published 60 years or so ago. The chances of finding the road through the village as free of cars as it is here, however, are remote.

The **Stoke Inn** at Chew Stoke, seen here on a postcard from the 1930s, was rebuilt in the late nineteenth century on the site of a much older building. While cycling though Chew Stoke on 29 August 1906, Cecil Sharp met 64-year-old William Stokes, who sang him one of the most haunting of English folk songs, The Streams of Lovely Nancy. Stone built and deceptively spacious, the Stoke Inn has two bars, a restaurant and a skittle alley, and also offers accommodation for people flying out of nearby Bristol Airport – a role Sharp could never have dreamt of as he sat listening to William Stokes on that long-gone summer evening.

Stephen Speed was the landlord of the **Crown** at West Harptree when it appeared on this postcard in 1911. The Crown – and St Mary's church – are still there, although the outbuilding to the left of the pub has made way for a car park. The architect and antiquarian John Wood, who believed that large tracts of north Somerset had once been settled by Druids, claimed that the village got its name from their habit of hanging their harps on trees in the neighbourhood. The chances that he picked up the story from a mischievous local drinking cider outside the Crown seem high. The village's name actually means 'the military road by the wood'.

An early example of flying the flag is seen on a postcard from around 1905 of the **King's Arms** in Litton, although back then it would have been for a jubilee or some such occasion rather than football on a plasma screen. Believed to date from the fifteenth century, this large Mendip inn has seen few external changes since this card was published. A window has been inserted in the expanse of wall behind the man on the right and a porch has been added to the doorway on the left, but that is about all. Today, the King's Arms, with a riverside terrace, is not only a popular dining pub, but also hosts folk and jazz evenings.

The scattered parish of Penselwood, hard against the Wiltshire border, once had three beerhouses – the Rest & Be Thankful on Pen Lane, which closed in 1926, the King's Arms on Coombe Street, which closed in 1910, and the Queen's Head, also on Coombe Street, which closed in 1975. Now all that is left is the Hunter's Lodge a couple of miles away on the main road. The **Queen's Head** is seen here on a postcard from around 1910. During the Second World War, with army camps and an airfield nearby, the Queen's Head was very busy. Among those who looked in was Lt-Col David Niven of the Rifle Brigade who was stationed at Stourton.

An extension has been tacked onto the **Bell** at Leigh on Mendip, but, apart from that, and the addition of some fancy shutters, this pub, with its seventeenth-century mullion windows, looks much the same as it did when this postcard was published around 1910. Leigh is a place where drinking seems to have been taken seriously. In 1857, a new vicar, keen on temperance, came to the parish. Mounting the pulpit one Sunday to expatiate on his favourite hobby-horse, one of the parishioners pulled out a gun and fired. Fortunately, he was a poor shot – the result of too much cider, perhaps – and the vicar sustained only minor injuries.

No, not a rogue page from Narrow Gauge Railways of Yesteryear – this is how beer from Oakhill Brewery started out on its journey to the pub. The brewery at Oakhill, high in the Mendips north of Shepton Mallet, was established in 1767 and by the end of the nineteenth century was shipping out up to 2500 barrels a week via the railhead at Binegar, two miles away. The traction engines which carried the beer there were ripping up the roads to such an extent that the district council ordered the brewery to find an alternative means of transport. And so, in 1903, the only narrow-gauge brewery railway in the country was built.

The line was operated by two locomotives - Oakhill, seen above on the viaduct at Binegar Bottom, and Mendip, seen in the brewery yard. It lasted for only 18 years, lorries taking over its duties in 1921. In 1925, the brewery suffered a disastrous fire and was taken over by Bristol United Breweries. If the railway – and the brewery – had somehow survived, it would surely have been one of the county's top tourist attractions. As it is, all we can do is try to imagine what it must have been like standing in the brewery yard early one winter's morning, with noise and bustle all around, and the smell of malt and steam mingling in the air.

Cranmore was originally known as 'Crane Mere' or the Lake of the Cranes, a reminder that you were likely to get your feet wet if you wandered around Somerset much in the old days. There were, of course, certain compensations, and this was one of them – the **Strode Arms**, seen here on a postcard from around 1906. The mere may have shrunk to a duckpond, but the inn, named after the lords of the manor, is still in business, with regular listings in the Good Beer and Good Pub Guides. And, if, having seen the pictures on the previous page, you're hankering after the days of steam, the East Somerset Railway is a mere whistle toot away.

When the railway reached Woodborough on the Cheddar Valley line in 1869, the nearby Packhorse Inn was renamed the **Woodbrough Railway Commercial Inn**. Here the landlord and his friends pose with the new sign. Within a few months, the station took the name of Winscombe, the adjoining village, to avoid confusion with Woodborough station in Wiltshire. The railway closed in 1963, but the inn, rebuilt in the 1930s and now known as the Woodborough Inn, is still going strong. The houses in the background, to the north of the inn, have also survived, helping to pinpoint the spot where this photograph was taken.

A century ago, nobody gave a second thought to children playing – or simply standing – in the road, but within a few years the advent of the internal combustion engine had put paid to something which had always seemed perfectly natural. The world was suddenly a more dangerous place and childhood pleasures that much more proscribed. This is the scene in Wanstrow, between Bruton and Frome, around 1905. The **Wanstrow Inn**, on the corner, is long closed, but the Good Beer Guide-listed Pub at Wanstrow, a few doors down, has taken over its mantle, serving fine food and wine, along with beers from nearby Blindman's Brewery.

Hilda Newton was working at the **Seymour Arms** in Witham Friary when she sent this postcard of the pub to her sister at Mere in September 1906. Virtually unchanged, today the Seymour Arms is as fine an example of an unspoilt local as you're likely to find anywhere. Service is through a hatch in the hallway, with beer and Burrow Hill cider straight from the barrel. The building dates from 1866, when the old Red Lion, which once stood on the site, was pulled down by the Duke of Somerset as part of a improvement scheme.

Now renamed the Bull Terrier and with a listing in the Good Beer Guide, the **Rose & Crown** at Croscombe, with its stone-flagged floors and inglenook fireplaces, dates back to 1612. Removal of render has revealed that, while the bay and the part of the building to its right is of ashlar stone, the rest is rubble stone. The thirteenth-century market cross was the scene of a famous battle in 1870, when the council decided to move it and accidentally broke the shaft. Villagers attacked the workmen, driving them away, and 30 men camped around the cross until the authorities agreed it could stay. A more orderly gathering is seen on this postcard from around 1910.

Today, the **Fountain Inn**, on St Thomas Street in Wells, is a thriving gastropub, home to Boxer's Restaurant and with its own wine club. One could be forgiven for thinking it has an illustrious history. Certainly its ashlar-stone facade and generous proportions indicate it was one of Wells' top coaching inns until the trade disappeared in the mid-1800s. By the end of the century, its location at the edge of town, on a road now used only by locals, had led to an almost complete collapse of trade. John Hawkes, the landlord in 1894, got most of his income from working as a blacksmith. He was succeeded by Henry Simmons, who tried to make a living from the inn alone. When he left, the inn closed, and Frederick Stanton, seen here around 1912, ran a boot and shoe repair business from the premises for many years. A fire at some stage during the twentieth century marked another downturn in the old inn's fortunes – but, in a book which laments the loss of so many inns, it is good to feature one that has come so triumphantly back from the dead.

The **Swan Inn**, on Sadler Street in the heart of Wells, suffered no such downturn in its fortunes. This coaching inn, immortalised in the film Hot Fuzz, dates from the sixteenth century, if not earlier, but was refronted in the late eighteenth or early nineteenth century, so that it bears more than a passing resemblance to the Fountain. Since this postcard was published around a century ago, the archway leading to the coachyard has been widened to accommodate cars and the shop with the canted bays on the right has been remodelled, but otherwise little has changed.

Just across the road from the entrance to Wookey Hole Caves, the **Wookey Hole Inn**, with its mix of rubble stone and half timbering, could hardly fail to be successful. Happily, though, this is no lowest-common-denominator, fleece-the-grockles excuse for a decent pub. With a listing in the Good Beer Guide, wacky decor, jazz, Mediterranean and 'fusion' cuisine, beer festivals, and eight Belgian beers on draught, it may not be your traditional idea of a country pub, but it's certainly not turned its back on the brewer's art. And it still looks much as it did when this postcard was published in the 1920s.

Keinton Mandeville was the birthplace, in 1838, of John Brodribb, who, after changing his name to Henry Irving, became one of the nineteenth century's greatest actors. The **Three Old Castles Inn**, in the heart of the village, is somewhat hidden away in this 1920s postcard view, but the delivery lorry from Brutton's Brewery gives an added interest to the scene. The Three Old Castles is still going strong, but Bruttons was absorbed into Brutton, Mitchell, Tomms Ltd in 1937. The Charlton Brewery of Shepton Mallet, which owned the Three Old Castles, was taken over by Bristol United Breweries the same year.

Shepton Mallet's Market Square can rarely have been as packed as it was when this photograph was taken. It probably shows the results of one of 1910's two General Elections being announced. These were turbulent times, and no doubt arguments and recriminations continued long after the voters' verdicts were delivered. The **Black Swan**, one of Shepton's oldest hostelries, was handily placed to slake throats parched with cheering – or to fuel resentment at the result. The Black Swan was demolished in the 1970s to make way for Boot's, at the same time as the buildings beyond it were demolished to make way for the Amulet – now the Academy – Theatre.

Two more of Shepton Mallet's lost inns feature on these early twentieth-century postcards: the **George**, on the right, is now the Midland Bank; below, men of the North Somerset Yeomanry line up outside the **Hare & Hounds** on the corner of High Street and Commercial Street. The fate of the Hare & Hounds was particularly sad. Demolished in the 1960s, it was replaced by a Co-op store in a style that, even by the architectural standards of the day, was particularly brutal.

Wincanton was not only an important coaching town but also had, in Nathaniel Ireson, an outstanding local architect. After building Stourhead to Colen Campbell's designs in the 1720s, he turned his attention to Wincanton's inns. The **Dolphin**, originally the Rainbow, was built of rubble stone with ashlar dressings. When this postcard was published in the 1920s, the Dolphin was owned by Matthews' Brewery of Gillingham. Matthews' closed in 1963 after acquisition by Hall & Woodhouse, but in 2005 a new Matthews' Brewery – with no connection to the old one – opened at Timsbury near Bath.

First recorded as an inn in 1655, the **White Horse** was rebuilt by Ireson in 1733. When the railways came, just over a century later, Wincanton's economy, dependent on the coaching trade, collapsed. In the late nineteenth century, an enterprising businessman set up a milk-drying plant in the old coachyard at the back of White Horse, producing the first powdered milk in the country. When doctors acclaimed the new product as a miracle food for babies, the business took off, and Wincanton became home to the Cow & Gate Creamery. The White Horse, like the Dolphin, is still open.

Today, Pilton is famous as the home of Europe's biggest music festival. Until the Somerset Levels were drained, however, it was an inland port where, according to legend, Joseph of Arimathea landed in the first century. The **Crown Inn** dates from the 1600s and was once the tap for the White Hart, which occupied the building on the left, now partly occupied by the village store. As this pair of photographs show, the only significant change in the last 70 years has been the remodelling of the roof on the old White Hart.

Originally known as the Cock, the **Crown Inn** in Bruton stood on the banks of the River Brue near Church Bridge. Until a flood prevention scheme was implemented in the 1980s, this part of town was particularly hard hit by flash floods which occurred in the summer when the ground was baked hard and rainwater from sudden downpours ran straight off the hills into the river. Given such regular inundations, the demolition of the Crown in the 1960s was, although regrettable, hardly surprising.

Men of the Army Service Corps line up outside the **Ring of Bells** at Hinton Blewitt some time during the First World War. They were probably serving with the 134th Motor Transport Company, which was based at Wells in 1916. The curious thing about the picture is that, although the men are standing outside a pub, very few of them seem to be drinking. This probably had more to do with the chronic shortage of beer during the First World War than the soldiers' reluctance to sample the local ale. Coombs' Breweries, which owned the Ring of Bells, was acquired by Oakhill Brewery in 1922, but the Ring of Bells, with a listing in the Good Beer Guide, is still a very popular village pub. And, with the church behind it and the rolling hills of Somerset in front, its situation is one of the finest in Somerset.

The imposing building on the right in this postcard view from around 1910 was the **New Inn** at Camerton. Built around 1800, it originally stood alongside the Somerset Coal Canal, offering accommodation and brewing its own beer. When the GWR built a railway along the line of the canal a century later, access to the pub was via a low bridge under the line – so low that brewery drays could not negotiate it and barrels had to be rolled the final part of their journey by hand. The pub, later renamed the Jolly Collier, survived not only the canal, but also the railway and the nearby collieries, although it has recently become a private house. The area in front of it, including the trackbed of the old line, is now covered by a housing estate.

A Lamb Brewery lorry stands outside Welshmill Works in Frome, carrying a brewing copper destined for a Belgian brewery destroyed in the First World War. Welshmill Works, founded by James Oxley in the mid-nineteenth century, was one of the biggest manufacturers of brewing equipment in the country. William Wilson, Oxley's manager, later took over the business. He was also part owner of a similar factory on the other side of town called Wilson & Scotchman's. In 1858, James Oxley designed the Lamb Brewery in Frome, one of the largest in Somerset. The timing of its opening – just eight years after the railway arrived – was significant. Before the arrival of the railway, Frome, with poor transport links, would have been unable to support such a major enterprise. As it was, when the brewery opened there was a pool of cheap labour in the town. Frome's wealth had been based on weaving, which was decimated by rapid mechanisation of the weaving industry in the north of England, leading to high unemployment. Today there is little left of the two sites where brewing equipment was made. Part of the Lamb Brewery, which closed in 1957, however, has been converted to residential use, while the old brewery tap – the Lamb Inn – is now the brewery tap for Blindman's Brewery from nearby Leighton

The landlord of the **Sun Inn** in Catherine Street stands outside the pub in this 1950s view. Today, the render has been stripped from the walls of this seventeenth-century building in one of Frome's best preserved streets, revealing the golden rubble stone beneath. Dating from the time when Frome was the largest town in Somerset after Bath, its Cotswold-style gables are characteristic of many old buildings in the town. The original Sun Inn stood a little way along the street. It was demolished in 1812 to make way for an extension to the Baptist chapel and the licence was transferred to the current premises.

The **White Hart**, one of the largest properties on Cheap Street in Frome, dated from the sixteenth century. A new façade was added in the eighteenth century and, by the time this postcard was published around 1910, further changes, such as the addition of bays to the first-floor windows, had been made. More were to follow when the inn closed and was converted to a shop. Cheap Street was the site of Frome's first market (Cheap was the Old English word for market); the spring which still runs down the middle of the street was no doubt handy for carrying away the rubbish generated by a medieval market.

The **George** in Frome, first recorded in 1650, has seen many changes of fortune. When it was refronted around 1750, it was one of the town's top inns. In 1874, having been run by the same landlord for 40 years, it was on the point of collapse and had to be virtually rebuilt. The classical portico, seen on this postcard from around 1906, went during the First World War when an army lorry ran out of control. By the 1970s, the inn was once again in a parlous state and closed for an extended period. There was talk of demolition, but fortunately it has been saved once again, and now looks in even better shape than it did a century ago.

A Railway Workers' May Day Parade passes the **Ship** in Frome in 1918. Although the war still had over six months to run, the country was being convulsed by wave after wave of industrial action as food prices rose ever higher. Today, the Ship has become the Olive Tree and, although it looks much the same, regulars from a century – or even a decade – ago would find it difficult to come to terms with the Tomato & Feta Parcels, Chargrilled Asparagus and Stilton & Stout Paté that have replaced the pickled eggs. An imaginative make-over – with the site of the building to the left transformed into a secluded garden – have made this one of the chicest places in town.

The **Bell** at Standerwick, on the busy A36, started life as a coaching inn. There have been many changes since this postcard was published a century ago – and not just to the volume of traffic. The front door has been blocked up and replaced by a window and a large extension to accommodate diners has been added at the side. Yet, although the customers seen on this card might find it difficult to reconcile the inn they knew with today's hostelry, its original function – of serving good ale, wine and food to locals and travellers alike – has not really changed that much.

The **Woolpack** at Beckington is another popular dining pub. Dating from the sixteenth century, but rebuilt in the eighteenth, its name recalls the trade that was the bedrock of the local economy until the early nineteenth century. The A36 once passed through the village, but a bypass has now taken the constant stream of cars and lorries away from the village, restoring some of the tranquillity glimpsed on this postcard from the 1920s.

When this postcard of the **New Inn** at Faulkland was published shortly before the First World War, most country people's choice of transport was limited to cycling, riding a horse or walking. The rise in car ownership in the second half of the twentieth century has not only transformed the fortunes of villages like Faulkland but also redefined the character and function of country pubs. How could Mr Hale, standing proudly outside his pub and flanked by his family, have foreseen that, less than a century later, most of the New Inn's customers would turn up by car? Unusually, both of Faulkland's pubs are still open. The New Inn, an imposing eighteenth-century rubble-stone building with ashlar dressings and a broad, single-storey canted porch, stands near the village green, while Tucker's Grave, a roadside beerhouse unchanged for a century or more, is a mile eastwards on the way to Norton St Philip.

Edward Keel was not only the landlord of the **Wagon & Horses** at Peasedown St John but also the owner of the Peasedown Brewery. This postcard view gives a good idea what this nineteenth-century mining village, six miles south-west of Bath, was like in the early 1900s. There are few houses and the only thing on the road, apart from some passers-by, is a cart laden with coal and presumably headed for Bath. The pub is still open, but looks very different: its ashlar stone has been painted white, a walled beer garden occupies the forecourt, the doorway on the corner has been replaced by a window, the cast-iron urinal by a porch, and the plate glass by leaded lights. Peasedown has changed almost beyond recognition as well. The collieries which brought it into being closed in the 1950s, but Peasedown, far from dwindling away, has continued to expand as a dormitory town for Bath, while the road, as empty as far as the eye can see in this Edwardian view, has grown so busy that a by-pass has had to be built.

Rode was once one of the most important weaving centres in Somerset. It also had several coaching inns and a large brewery in the centre of the village. The brewery closed in 1962, but its buildings, now converted to flats, can still be seen behind the Cross Keys Inn. Facing the Cross Keys, on the other side of the road, was the **Red Lion Inn**, dating from the eighteenth century, and seen here in the 1930s with the landlord, James Martin, at the door. Although little changed, today the Red Lion is a private house.

A similar fate has befallen the **George Inn**, a few doors along from the Red Lion, seen here on a postcard from 1908. The scene is still recognisable today, although a hedge now blocks the entrance to the forecourt of the inn and a new house has been built on the right. Rode, like many Somerset towns and villages, experienced a dramatic decline in population during the nineteenth century. In 1801, it had 927 inhabitants, most of them employed in the town's mills. A century later, the figure had fallen to 463. In recent years, however, as Rode has taken on a new role as a dormitory town, the population has climbed back up to around 850.

Albert Yeates, born in Beckington in 1855, served as a colour sergeant at the Royal Military Asylum in Chelsea before returning to Somerset to run the **Mason's Arms** at Marston Gate near Frome. On this postcard from around 1906, two draymen are seen outside the pub. Today, greatly extended, the Mason's Arms is one of the most popular dining pubs in the area.

The **Mason's Arms** in Hinton Charterhouse, four miles south of Bath, was tucked away down Green Lane, on the way to the church. A beerhouse, it survived until the 1950s, and villagers can still remember singalongs in its cosy bar, with the local vicar joining in the proceedings. The building, dating from the eighteenth century, is now a private house. Blake's Brewery from Trowbridge, which owned the Mason's Arms when this postcard was published shortly before the First World War, was taken over by Usher's in 1922.

Hinton Charterhouse's two other pubs have both survived. The **Stag** only had a beerhouse licence when James Smith ran it in the early 1900s. Today it is fully licensed, and, although popular for food, it is still very much a village pub. Apart from the application of limewash to both ashlar and rubble-stone walls, the fitting of some impressive stained glass to the ground-floor windows and the conversion of the openings on the right to windows, the Stag has changed very little in the intervening century.

Hinton Charterhouse got its name from a Carthusian priory that once stood nearby. On the old road from Bath to Salisbury, the **Crown** was a well-known staging post for centuries. The old inn, which stood on the site occupied, in this early twentieth-century view, by a water tank, burnt down in the 1880s when sparks from a traction engine set fire to its thatched roof. The building that replaced it – now known as the Rose & Crown – has recently been acquired by Butcombe Brewery. Although extended at the back and now offering accommodation, from the front it looks the same as it did a century ago. The water tank, however, has made way for a car park.

The **Globe Inn** at Newton St Loe, first recorded in 1725, stood at the point where the turnpike roads from Bath to Bristol and Wells diverged. The inn survived the loss of the coaching trade and got a new lease of life in the early twentieth century when Bath Electric Tramways opened a line to the inn. On this postcard from around 1910, a tram has just arrived from town and a group of passengers are heading towards the inn. The trams were withdrawn in 1938, and, although the inn is still recognisable today, its surroundings, which now include a dual carriageway and a large – and very busy – roundabout, have changed beyond recognition.

The **Lamb & Lark** in Keynsham High Street, seen here in the late 1930s, opened on 20 March 1745 with William Thomas as the landlord. He was also an excise officer, and the inn continued to be an excise office until the early twentieth century. It was taken over by George's in 1909 and closed in the 1960s. It was demolished without warning one Sunday morning in 1970. Its loss effectively ripped the heart out of the town and heralded the start of the Sack of Keynsham.

The solemn young man standing by the locks at Keynsham lends a wistful air to this Edwardian view of the **White Hart Inn** – now the Lock Keeper. The River Avon Navigation, which made the river navigable as far upstream as Bath, opened in 1727, and the White Hart opened around the same time. Situated on the north bank of the river, it is actually in South Gloucestershire, but, as it's generally regarded as being in Keynsham, we decided it should feature here, albeit in an honorary capacity. Keynsham was named after St Keyne, the daughter of a fifth century Welsh king who came over to England to live as a hermit on the banks of the Avon. Having got rid of the snakes which infested the area – by turning them to stone – she became something of a celebrity and travelled widely in the West Country. Now owned by Wells & Young's of Bedford, the Lock Keeper's situation, with a canalside beer garden, makes it deservedly popular.

Over on the other side of Bath, members of the Harbutt family from Bathampton (of plasticine fame) pose for a group portrait outside the **Fox** at Midford, between Hinton Charterhouse and Bath. In the early days of motoring, only the upper-middle classes could afford a vehicle like this. Even so, breakdowns were common, which probably explains why they brought the horse-drawn carriage along as well. How could they have foreseen that a century later there would be a constant stream of traffic past this former inn, with no need of horses in case of breakdowns, and that any attempt to recreate this scene today would risk at best a stream of irate drivers, at worst serious injury? The Fox closed over 60 years ago, but traces of the advertising roundel partially obscured by the car can still be seen today.

There is no better place to end our tour of Somerset's historic inns than the **George** in Norton St Philip. During refurbishment in 1998, tests established that the trees used to construct the roof and timber frame were felled in 1431. This was, however, a rebuild of an earlier building. Built by the monks of nearby Charterhouse Priory, the George was a centre for the woollen and weaving trades for centuries, with the inn serving as both warehouse and auction room. On 26 June 1685, with the monks long departed and the wool trade under the control of local grandees, the George was catapulted to the forefront of national affairs when the Duke of Monmouth, six days after declaring himself king at Taunton, arrived at the inn. By then, however, his campaign to wrest the crown from James II had all but run out of steam. Having failed to take Bristol, and with Bath closed against him, he had, despite a successful skirmish against the King's forces in the lanes around Norton St Philip, little option but to retreat. Ten days later, in the early hours of 7 July, his dreams of glory were finally snuffed out amid the rhynes and ditches of Sedgemoor. In a trial at the George a few weeks later, the infamous Judge Jefferies sentenced twelve local men to hang on the village common for their alleged part in the rebellion.

The pictures on the left and the one on the opposite page date from the 1880s when a party of antiquarians visited the George Inn. The view of the bar above was published by John Chard, landlord of the George in the 1930s. Mansford & Baily, whose names appear on the advertisement, were wine and spirit merchant's on Bath Street in Frome. Although carts bearing coal from the North Somerset coalfield no longer call at the inn, and although Mansford & Baily have long gone, such changes as there have been at the George have preserved its unique character as one of England's most historic and atmospheric inns.

A great comfort to me has been Wiveliscombe Old Ale. I have had half a pint every night for 70 years; it gives me strength and sleep

Beer advertising hasn't always been about lads downing lager. Years before Guinness was good for you or Bernard Miles told you that Mackeson looked good, tasted good, and (by golly) did you good, Hancock's of Wiveliscombe – the largest brewery in the south-west – trundled out Betty Bushen of Minehead to promote the health-giving quality of their old ale. Pity they didn't wake her up for the photo shoot. In 1927, Hancock's merged with Arnold & Sons of Taunton, and closed after being taken over by Usher's in the 1950s. Today, Wiveliscombe is home to two new breweries – Exmoor, housed in part of the old Hancock's building, and Cotleigh.

CYDER MAKING

Much has been made, in the preceding pages, of the long-forgotten breweries that once graced the county; there has been little mention of what many regard as a more important part of Somerset's alcoholic heritage – farmhouse cider. To go some way towards redressing the balance, our final postcard shows cider – or cyder – making on Kimber's Farm around 1906. The exact location is unknown, as there were Kimbers farming in both Charlton Musgrove and Stoke Trister. Happily, while local breweries had to wait for the real-ale revival before staging a comeback, small-scale production of farmhouse cider never died out.